Mississippi Observed

Mississippi Observed

Photographs from the Photography Collection
of the Mississippi Department of Archives and History
with Selections from Literary Works by Mississippians

*Photographs Selected and Edited by
Sheree Hightower and Cathie Stanga*

Text Selected and Edited by Carol Cox

UNIVERSITY PRESS OF MISSISSIPPI   JACKSON

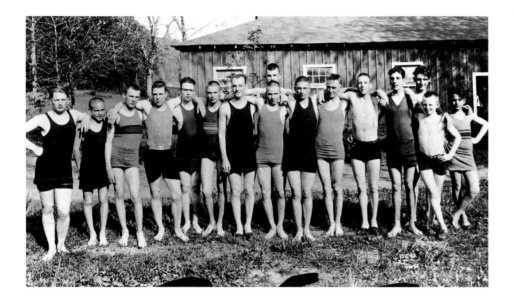

97 96 95 94 4 3 2 1

The paper in this book meets the guidelines for perma-
nence and durability of the Committee on Production
Guidelines for Book Longevity of the Council on Library
Resources.

Library of Congress Cataloging-in-Publication Data

Mississippi observed / photographs selected and edited by
    Sheree Hightower and Cathie Stanga ; text selected and
    edited by Carol Cox.
        p. cm.
    ISBN 0-87805-727-7
    1. Mississippi—Pictorial works. 2. Mississippi—
Description and travel. I. Hightower, Sheree. II. Stanga,
Cathie. III. Cox, Carol, 1946- .
F342.M47 1994
976.2—dc20   94−19079
                                                        CIP

British Library Cataloging-in-Publication data available

Photograph captions begin on page 136
Acknowledgments begin on page 142

It is by knowing where you stand that you grow able to judge where you are. Place absorbs our earliest notice and attention, it bestows on us our original awareness; and our critical powers spring up from the study of it and the growth of experience inside it. It perseveres in bringing us back to earth when we fly too high. It never really stops informing us, for it is forever astir, alive, changing, reflecting, like the mind of man itself. One place comprehended can make us understand other places better. Sense of place gives equilibrium; extended, it is sense of direction too. Carried off we might be in spirit, and should be, when we are reading or writing something good; but it is the sense of place going with us still that is the ball of golden thread to carry us there and back and in every sense of the word to bring us home.

EUDORA WELTY

PREFACE

There are images—especially, it seems, to Southerners—that never go away; they do not even fade.

ELIZABETH SPENCER

As the twentieth century turns into the twenty-first, this book presents lingering glimpses of Mississippi just before and after the nineteenth century gave way to the present one. Here in these pages time and place are observed through the lenses of photographers, both amateur and professional, whose images have been collected and preserved by the Mississippi Department of Archives and History. From the works in this collection the editors have selected photographs depicting every geographical region of the state and a wide range of social and ethnic groups and activities; identification of the pictures appears in the back of this book.

The photographs are enhanced by commentary and narrative from the published works of many acclaimed Mississippi writers of the twentieth century. Thirty-six writers are represented in this volume:

Larry Brown, Will Campbell, Turner Cassity, Ellen Douglas, William Faulkner, Shelby Foote, Richard Ford, Ellen Gilchrist, Barry Hannah, Brooks Haxton, Beth Henley, Rebecca Hill, Kenneth Holditch, T. R. Hummer, Angela Jackson, Beverly Lowry, Berry Morgan, Willie Morris, Lewis Nordan, Walker Percy, William Alexander Percy, Sterling Plumpp, Susan Prospere, James Seay, Edgar Simmons, Elizabeth Spencer, Clifton Taulbert, Mildred Taylor, Margaret Walker, Jerry W. Ward, Jr., Eudora Welty, James Whitehead, Tennessee Williams, Richard Wright, Al Young, and Stark Young.

Through their observations we perceive and appreciate the state's brooding natural beauty, the people and towns and countrysides, Mississippi's complex and omnipresent past, and its indwelling power to sustain and inspire. In the juxtaposition of these archival pictures and the writing that came later lies a profound reminder of Mississippi's distinctive sense of place. This imprint may be the enduring signature of atmosphere and the slant of light, of memory and the human heart.

Publication of this volume

was made possible by

BOOKFRIENDS

the Associates of the

University Press of Mississippi

Mississippi Observed

At first there had been only the old towns along the River and the old towns along the hills, from each of which the planters with their gangs of slaves and then of hired laborers had wrested from the impenetrable jungle of water-standing cane and cypress, gum and holly and oak and ash, cotton patches which as the years passed became fields and then plantations. The paths made by deer and bear became roads and then highways, with towns in turn springing up along them and along the rivers Tallahatchie and Sunflower which joined and became the Yazoo, the River of the Dead of the Choctaws—the thick, slow, black, unsunned streams almost without current, which once each year ceased to flow at all and then reversed, spreading, drowning the rich land and subsiding again, leaving it still richer.

Most of that was gone now. Now a man drove two hundred miles from Jefferson before he found wilderness to hunt in. Now the land lay open from the cradling hills on the East to the rampart of levee on the West, standing horseman-tall with cotton for the world's looms—the rich black land, imponderable and vast, fecund up to the very doorsteps of the negroes who worked it and of the white men who owned it; which exhausted the hunting life of a dog in one year, the working life of a mule in five and of a man in twenty—the land in which neon flashed past them from the little countless towns and countless shining this-year's automobiles sped past them on the broad plumb-ruled highways, yet in which the only permanent mark of man's occupation seemed to be the tremendous gins, constructed in sections of sheet iron and in a week's time though they were, since no man, millionaire though he be, would build more than a roof and walls to shelter the camping equipment he lived from when he knew that once each ten years or so his house would be flooded to the second storey and all within it ruined; —the land across which there came now no scream of panther but instead the long hooting of locomotives: trains of incredible length and drawn by a single engine, since there was no gradient anywhere and no elevation save those raised by forgotten aboriginal hands as refuges from the yearly water and used by their Indian successors to sepulchre their fathers' bones, and all that remained of that old time were the Indian names on the little towns and usually pertaining to water—Aluschaskuna, Tillatoba, Homochitto, Yazoo.

WILLIAM FAULKNER

Sweet bay and cypress and sweetgum and live oak and swamp maple closing tight made the wall dense, and yet there was somewhere still for the other wall of vine; it gathered itself on the ground and stacked and tilted itself in the trees; and like a table in the tree the mistletoe hung up there black in the zenith. Buzzards floated from one side of the swamp to the other, as if choice existed for them—raggedly crossing the sky and shadowing the track, and shouldering one another on the solitary limb of a moon-white sycamore. Closer to the ear than lips could begin words came the swamp sounds— closer to the ear and nearer to the dreaming mind.

EUDORA WELTY

3

Across this wide flat alluvial stretch . . . run slowly and circuitously other rivers and creeks, also high-banked, with names pleasant to remember—Rattlesnake Bayou, Quiver River, the Bogue Phalia, the Tallahatchie, the Sunflower—pouring their tawny waters finally into the Yazoo, which in turn loses itself just above Vicksburg in the river. With us when you speak of "the river," though there are many, you mean always the same one, the great river, the shifting unappeasable god of the country, feared and loved, the Mississippi.

WILLIAM ALEXANDER PERCY

NATCHEZ UNDER THE HILL

. . . so that the steamboats carrying the baled cotton to Memphis or New Orleans seemed to crawl along the sky itself.

WILLIAM FAULKNER

He had known the river was there, having heard Duff speak of it and having seen it on the map, but 'river' to him meant the rivers of New England, France, and Italy; he had expected to find a village sprawled along its bank, all green and peaceful, with white church spires and cottages in ordered rows, each with its brass knocker. . . . He would have been even more dismayed, and perhaps alarmed, if he had known that instead of the town overlooking the river, the river— from behind its earthwork, which he did not recognize; he saw no sign of the river at all—overlooked the town.

SHELBY FOOTE

The stageplank was taken in on schedule. The paddle blades thrashed water, backing the steamer away from the wharf; the whistle screamed and rumbled, precipitating steam, and the paddles reversed, driving the boat ahead on the forward slope of a churning wave. From the rail Duff watched Bristol shrink and fade in the pale light of the winter dawn. When he was a mile downriver the sun rose big and scarlet, and as the steamboat rounded the lower bend he looked back and saw the town gleam blood-red for an instant, house roofs and church spires, smoke stacks and water towers burgeoning in flame. Then, apparitionlike, as the trees along the Arkansas bank swept a curtain of green across it, it was gone.

SHELBY FOOTE

She and Anna stood looking around. Wilderness was all about them. As far as they could see on either side of the lake not even a road ran down to the water's edge. While they watched, two white herons dragged themselves awkwardly into the air and flapped away, long legs trailing. Green and sand-colored plains, which in the spring had been a part of the bottom of the lake, now swept up and back a quarter of a mile to the rise of the levee. The ground was marked every hundred or so yards with a wavy line like the high-tide line on a beach, which, when one drew closer, turned out to be tangles of driftwood, laid down in undulating bands where the lake had paused in its steady summer drop. Clumps of cottonwood and sycamore trees rose here and there from hummocks of grassy sand which earlier in the summer had been islands in the broad expanse of the lake. Ranks of willows, fringed from top to bottom with delicate, feathery fronds and banded with water marks, thrust their spindly trunks thirty, forty, or fifty feet into the air, taller the farther back they stood from the lake.

ELLEN DOUGLAS

In the uncertain season between late winter and early spring of that year it rained without letup in Eunola for nineteen straight days. Night and day, heavy, splashing drops. In that time, yards were turned into small lakes and houses were isolated from one another like stones on a field. Dampness crept inside, mildewing shoes, swelling windows and joints to cranky stiffness, and rain drenched every newly planted spring garden, washing out sprouted seeds, slim stalks, thready roots, floating topsoil away. It was a crucial season: farmers sat in kitchens and on back porches drinking coffee, waiting it out. Drains were full, ditches overflowing; children rowed boats through glassy intersections, as above them, traffic lights dumbly switched. The sound of rain falling became a daily rhythm which after a while went almost unnoticed, as life itself came to dwell inside the notion of its tock-tocks.

BEVERLY LOWRY

For thirty-six hours the Delta was in turmoil, in movement, in terror. Then the waters covered everything, the turmoil ceased, and a great quiet settled down; the stock which had not reached the levee had been drowned; the owners of second-story houses with their pantries and kitchens had moved upstairs; those in one-story houses had taken to the roofs and the trees. Over everything was silence, deadlier because of the strange cold sound of the currents gnawing at foundations, hissing against walls, creaming and clawing over obstructions.

WILLIAM ALEXANDER PERCY

If I could have one part of the world back the way it used to be, I would not choose Dresden before the fire bombing, Rome before Nero, or London before the blitz, I would not resurrect Babylon, Carthage or San Francisco. Let the leaning tower lean and the hanging gardens hang. I want the Mississippi Gulf Coast back the way it was before Hurricane Camille.

ELIZABETH SPENCER

. . . the sounds and smells of rural Mississippi breathe gently in on us. The crickets, the frogs, even—and this seems a touch theatrical, the South believing in itself again—one lone whippoorwill. . . . Evenings here are always the best, so calming after the jangling brilliance of sunlight, the heavy weight of humidity.

REBECCA HILL

The columns are enormously high and you can see some of the iron grillwork railing for the second-story gallery clinging halfway up. Vines cling to the fluted white plaster surfaces, and in some places the plaster has crumbled away, showing the brick underneath. Little trees grow up out of the tops of columns, and chickens have their dust holes among the rubble. . . . It is this ignorant way that the hand of Nature creeps back over Windsor that makes me afraid. I'd rather there'd be ghosts there, but there aren't. . . . When all of it was standing, back in the old days, it was higher even than the columns, and had a cupola, too. You could see the cupola from the river, they say, and the story went that Mark Twain used it to steer by. . . . What Nature does to Windsor it does to everything, including you and me—there's the horror.

ELIZABETH SPENCER

Half an hour north of Jackson on U. S. 49, not far
beyond the Big Black River, the casual rolling land
gives way to a succession of tall, lush hills, one after
another for twelve or fifteen miles. . . . On a quiet day
after a spring rain this stretch of earth seems prehis-
toric—damp, cool, inaccessible, the moss hanging
from the giant old trees. . . . Beyond these hills, if you
follow the highway as it forks north and slightly west,
the hills suddenly come to an end and there is one
long, final descent. Out in the distance, as far as the
eye can see, the land is flat, dark, and unbroken,
sweeping away in a faint misty haze to the limits of
the horizon. This is the great delta.

WILLIE MORRIS

The chickenyard scent of guano and dust soaked with dew rises
While all Earth is still,
Wind, pond water, dark woods,
Cloudless blue, green, rose depth in the East,
All still,
Except, inside the carpentered box, behind the rustic wooden latch,
The puck puck puck scream and loud beating of clipped wings
Invisibly made by the frizzly rooster with horrific regularity
As by the works of an apocalyptic metronome.

BROOKS HAXTON

In August
The pecan trees,
Taller than the local mansions,
Draw
From the remainder underground
Of ended seasons
The investment of the dead,
Deriving from lost leaves
And fallen catkins and old limbs
The terminal buds for another spring,
Provisioning the green shelves
Toward the fall bestowal
Of the latent seed.

BROOKS HAXTON

28

29

I love the land I was born to and I never tire of seeing the seasons and the weather change over it, or the hawks that sit high in the trees, or the rabbits that bound across the road, or the coons that band together in spring when they're rutting, or later at night, the owls that swoop low across the ditches or fly down to light in the road in front of you with mice caught in their talons, owls that glare at you with a hateful look before gathering their prey and swooping back up into a black and rainy night on their huge beating wings.

LARRY BROWN

30

34

Tonight, it was only the helpers, fishing. But their boat must be full of silver fish! Nina wondered if it was the slowness and near-fixity of boats out on the water that made them so magical. Their little boat in the reeds that day had not been far from this one's wonder, after all. The turning of water and sky, of the moon, or the sun, always proceeded, and there was this magical hesitation in their midst, of a boat. And in the boat, it was not so much that they drifted, as that in the presence of a boat the world drifted, forgot. The dreamed-about changed places with the dreamer. . . . Luminous of course but hidden from them, Moon Lake streamed out in the night. By moonlight sometimes it seemed to run like a river. . . . Here and there was the quicksand that stirred your footprint and kissed your heel. All snakes, harmless and harmful, were freely playing now; they put a trailing, moony division between weed and weed—bright, turning, bright and turning.

EUDORA WELTY

Most of the time, the fish that were caught were cooked for dinner or for supper. Occasionally, however, the fish became part of a fun-filled and festive Sunday afternoon. During those rare get-togethers, Ma Ponk would turn her house and yard into a park, and she and her friends would start early in the afternoon to get the fire hot. They would get the big black iron skillets red-hot and the grease would pop all over the place. There would be loaves and loaves of Wonder bread and the number-three tubs would be filled with cold Pabst Blue Ribbon and Jax beer. Ma Ponk's long front porch was turned into a stage where the local musicians would come to play and sing the blues, and her small front yard was soon filled with colored people.

CLIFTON TAULBERT

"There ain't a thing better than fish," muttered William Wallace. He lay stretched on his back in the glimmer and shade of trampled sand. His sunburned forehead and cheeks seemed to glow with fire. His eyelids fell. The shadow of a willow branch dipped and moved over him. "There is nothing in the world as good as . . . fish. The fish of Pearl River." Then slowly he smiled. He was asleep.

But it seemed almost at once that he was leaping up, and one by one up sat the others in their ring and looked at him, for it was impossible to stop and sleep by the river.

"You're feeling as good as you felt last night," said Virgil, setting his head on one side.

"The excursion is the same when you go looking for your sorrow as when you go looking for your joy," said Doc.

EUDORA WELTY

Almost every afternoon when the heat was not un-bearable my father and I would go out to the old baseball field behind the armory to hit flies. I would stand far out in center field, and he would station himself with a fungo at home plate, hitting me one high fly, or Texas Leaguer, or line drive after another, sometimes for an hour or more without stopping. . . . The smell of that new-cut grass was the finest of all smells, and I could run forever and never get tired. It was a dreamy, suspended state, those late afternoons, thinking of nothing but outfield flies as the world drifted lazily by on Jackson Avenue. . . . back home, even among the adults, baseball was all-meaning; it was the link with the outside.

WILLIE MORRIS

Coaches with their white sheer socks rolled down over their ankle bones, cheerleaders with those glossy green tights that have the red stripes on both sides, photographers, official timers, and the whole enemy bunch—including pious Revis—went scattering like leaves before a hurricane when I released myself into a signal flying body block at about the 50. . . . Being so much faster because of my big feet and overall im-mense energy, sweeping over the green grass like a surface-piercing hydrofoil-type speedboat, gliding along like the clippership *Nightingale*, I moved up along beside Royal—I came along beside and shouted: "Have no fear—Big Son is here!"

JAMES WHITEHEAD

And the blues, I tell you, they blew up
on target; blew the roof right off
& went whistling skyward, starward,
stilling every zooming one of us
mojo'd in the room that night, that
instant, that whenever-it-was. Torn
inside at first, we all got turned out,
twisting in a blooming space where
afternoon & evening fused like Adam
with Eve. The joyful urge to cry
mushroomed into a blinding cloudburst
of spirit wired for sound, then atomized
into one long, thunderous, cooling downpour.

AL YOUNG

The Deep South might be wretched, but it can howl.

BARRY HANNAH

Morning glories
Pull down music of work days,
Hometown, straw hat men
Walk with round women in ginghams.
I plow unfurrowed rows of my life:
Swinging in trees, sliding down hillsides,
And playing in cotton sheds.
My song of longing leaps
Through radios of your vistas
Like instant dreams in cups of sleep.
The mud and rains of freshness
Stroke my body like a do-right woman.
Black folks picking cotton
Hauling it to gins
Being cheated and whipped
Side their heads if complaints
Burst from sorghum lips.

STERLING D. PLUMPP

How did I first discover the color of my skin? I had only to look in my mirror every morning to know. I must say it appeared to me a good healthy color. But there is a difference in knowing you are black and in understanding what it means to be black in America. Before I was ten I knew what it was to step off the sidewalk to let a white man pass; otherwise he might knock me off. I had had a sound thrashing by white boys while Negro men looked on helplessly. I was accustomed to riding in the Jim-Crow street cars with the Negro section marked off by iron bars that could not be moved. For a year and a half I went to school in a one-room wooden shack. One year when my father's school work took him out of town constantly, my mother lived in fear of our lives because there was no man in the house to protect us against the possibility of some attack.

MARGARET WALKER

The summer inched through its humid hours. The figs on the trees along the chickenyard fence swelled up ("swole up," we said) and ripened and turned purple and fat. I played barefoot and barebacked in the shade of the broad fig leaves and sometimes picked the fruit from the limbs and watched the ooze of fig-milk from the stem as it covered my fingers. The figs were like soft wood on my tongue, and a sweet residue of poison hung in the Delta air, where the ditches had been sprayed for mosquitoes. . . . Some days my father brought home a watermelon, green-striped and big as a washtub, and the three of us, mother, father, and myself, cut it beneath the walnut tree and ate big seedy red wedges of melon in the metal lawnchairs.

Evenings my father fed the chickens—the Plymouth Rocks, the Rhode Island Reds, slow and fat and powdered with dust—and my mother made fig preserves and sealed the syrupy fruit in Mason jars with hot paraffin lids.

It is tempting to look back at this time and to remember only those images of ripeness and joy.

LEWIS NORDAN

And yet my mother, whom I loved and knew quite well, links me to that foreignness, that other thing that was her life and that I really don't know so much about and never did. This is one quality of our lives with our parents that is often overlooked and so, devalued. Parents link us—closeted as we are in our lives—to a thing we're not but they are; a separateness, perhaps a mystery—so that even together we are alone.

RICHARD FORD

MYRA: We used to go every night to the orchard across from Moon Lake. He used to say, "Love! Love! Love!" And so did I, and both of us meant it, I thought. But he quit me that summer for some aristocratic girl, a girl like Cassandra Whiteside! I seen a picture of them dancing together on the Peabody Roof in Memphis. Prominent planter's son and the debutante daughter of. . . . Of course, after that, what I really wanted was death.

TENNESSEE WILLIAMS

My father said swear to keep your feet
firmly on the ground, hold your head up, wear white
at night, always walk facing the traffic, whistle
while you work, finish anything you start, stick
with the same job so the boss sees you are loyal.

How I betrayed him.

Last time I saw his face he was holed up on the coast,
he had a room with a view, he said he spent the
    summer
spying on a hippie. He said, your cheeks look gaunt,
I wanted to say I love you but he strolled off
into the sea breeze. I saw his hands slide
into his pockets, heard his coins jangle against
his penknife. I bit my tongue. I didn't say
you don't eat right. I hated to see no matter
how he tightened his belt his hips were dried up
like a cow pond in a summer drought.

ELLEN GILCHRIST

In June there will be sweetheart roses
along the whitewashed fences.
Years ago I saw my father pin one on my mother
as if it were a corsage she would wear
to enter the evening.
Her body was limber then,
and the angels would have envied her had they
   seen her,
dancing in the Bahia grass a private dance
that did not include my father
or any of us who watched from an upstairs window.
This was the province of the sacred,
and we begged her with rising voices to come
   indoors.

SUSAN PROSPERE

Memory believes before knowing remembers.
W I L L I A M   F A U L K N E R

57

I began to marvel at how smoothly the black boys acted out the roles that the white race had mapped out for them. Most of them were not conscious of living a special, separate, stunted way of life. Yet I knew that in some period of their growing up—a period that they had no doubt forgotten—there had been developed in them a delicate, sensitive controlling mechanism that shut off their minds and emotions from all that the white race had said was taboo. Although they lived in an America where in theory there existed equality of opportunity, they knew unerringly what to aspire to and what not to aspire to.

RICHARD WRIGHT

On the porch of the yellow store, in her fresh stockings despite the heat, her toes eloquent in the white straps of her shoes, the elegant young lady waits. The men, two of them, look out to her occasionally. In the store, near a large reservoir, hang hooks, line, Cheetos, prophylactics, cream nougats. The roof of the store is tin. Around the woman the men, three decades older, see hot love and believe they can hear it speak from her ankles.

BARRY HANNAH

Like many young men in the South, he became overly subtle and had trouble ruling out the possible. They are not like an immigrant's son in Passaic who decides to become a dentist and that is that. Southerners have trouble ruling out the possible. What happens to a man to whom all things seem possible and every course of action open? Nothing of course. Except war. If a man lives in the sphere of the possible and waits for something to happen, what he is waiting for is war—or the end of the world. That is why Southerners like to fight and make good soldiers. In war the possible becomes actual through no doing of one's own.

WALKER PERCY

64

It was the middle of the great depression and Joe and I knew something wasn't right. Daddy had accepted a W.P.A. job but the rigidity and the discipline of it was more than he could take. He had never had someone tell him when to pick up a shovel before, when to put it down, which rock to move, when to begin, when to quit. When the rural poor, like the reservation Indians before them, were poured into a mold not of their own doing, one which made no sense except to foreman and timekeeper, they failed—and were known thereafter as lazy, shiftless, no-initiative "rednecks." For whatever reason, Daddy failed, quit, or was fired. . . . It was only when the depression came that we discovered we were, in fact, poor people. We were not destitute, not with cured hams and sides of bacon hanging in the smokehouse all year, chickens to lay eggs and to eat, cows to give us milk and butter, fields in which to grow food. Country people were not impoverished. They were simply poor.

WILL D. CAMPBELL

First the man explained that he was operating with a grant from Washington. This, we supposed, to indicate the magnitude of what he was about to say. He said the purpose of the grant was to rid our community of hookworms, adding that the South was backward, not so much because of the Civil War, but because of malaria and hookworms. (We had not known until then that we were backward and therefore had not pondered the possible reasons for our backwardness.)

WILL D. CAMPBELL

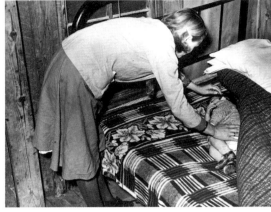

Ma Ponk and her friends, while turning multicolored scraps into treasured designs learned from their mothers and grandmothers, would laugh, talk, discuss their children and their northern relatives. Their calloused hands swiftly and expertly sewed their feelings of love into the fabric they had salvaged and saved. Many of these handmade quilts would later be boxed and sent north as gifts and warm reminders of family left behind.

CLIFTON TAULBERT

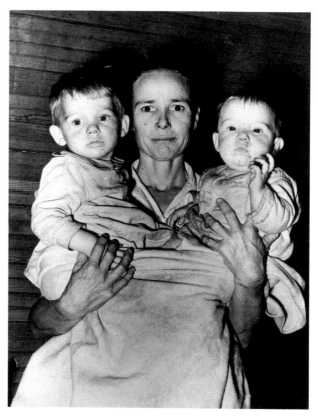

My mother and I look alike. Full, high forehead. The same chin, nose. There are pictures to show that. In myself I see her, even hear her laugh. In her life there was no particular brilliance, no celebrity. No heroics. No one crowning achievement to swell the heart. There were bad ones enough: a childhood that did not bear strict remembering; a husband she loved forever and lost; a life to follow that did not require comment. But somehow she made possible for me my truest affections, as an act of great literature would bestow upon its devoted reader.

RICHARD FORD

There are songs and there are story songs
Similar to the cold lungs of a star.
A poor boy needs the very thing he sings.

JAMES WHITEHEAD

When I was a boy, light moved
Off porches into twilight, and I ran
Deep into trees, into shadows,
Looking for what I thought was night
Until out of some distance
I had not been trying to forget
But had only lost
The voices came rising,
The voices of mothers telling me
Nothing but what I had
To remember across that space,
And I ran again, a boy
Who knew only he was running
Into himself, hearing
That name, that wind.

T. R. HUMMER

I hungered for the sharp, frightening, breath-taking, almost painful excitement that the story had given me, and I vowed that as soon as I was old enough I would buy all the novels there were and read them to feed that thirst for violence that was in me, for intrigue, for plotting, for secrecy, for bloody murders. . . .
I had tasted what to me was life, and I would have more of it, somehow, someway. . . . when no one was looking I would slip into Ella's room and steal a book and take it back of the barn and try to read it. Usually I could not decipher enough words to make the story have meaning. I burned to learn to read novels and I tortured my mother into telling me the meaning of every strange word I saw, not because the word itself had any value, but because it was the gateway to a forbidden and enchanting land. . . . I dreamed of going north and writing books, novels. . . . I was building up in me a dream which the entire educational system of the South had been rigged to stifle. I was feeling the very thing that the state of Mississippi had spent millions of dollars to make sure that I would never feel; I was becoming aware of the thing that the Jim Crow laws had been drafted and passed to keep out of my consciousness; I was acting on impulses that southern senators in the nation's capital had striven to keep out of Negro life; I was beginning to dream the dreams that the state had said were wrong, that the schools had said were taboo.

RICHARD WRIGHT

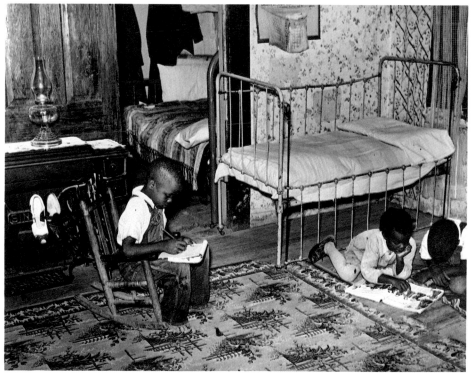

'Course, I never read many poems before. There
weren't all that many poem books you could get off
a the traveling bookmobile. Most books I got was
about animals. Farm animals, jungle animals, arctic
animals and such. 'Course they was informative, I
learned some things; they's called: a gaggle a geese;
a pride a lions; a warren a rabbits; a host a whales.
That's my personal favorite one: a host a whales!

BETH HENLEY

74

I saw tears in the old church as a child. I saw men cry, not only women. And at the pulpit I saw the only man I knew to shout in public. Sunday after Sunday, Brother Shepherd would rage at his church, go brilliant red from the shirt collar gripping his throat, and rasp out warnings and pleas and verses and truths in his cigarette-tarnished voice. The congregation was small; Brother Shepherd also had a job at the lumber mill four nights a week to provide for his family. But there was no question that he had the call for doing the work of the Lord in the daylight hours.

REBECCA HILL

There was a strong work ethic when I was growing up in the South. Every colored person worked from the time he was old enough to drag a sack through the cotton fields. The work was back breaking, exhausting and sometimes degrading. It often required a mother to leave home in the morning to go prepare breakfast for a white family before her own children were fed. Everybody worked, because in spite of everything, most of the older people still clung fast to the belief that if you worked hard, you would get a slice of the American dream.

CLIFTON TAULBERT

I ain't never been scared of hard work.
I useta be a longshoreman on the levees
and sometimes when I was laid off
I useta break strikes, you know
what they calls a scab.
I dug ditches and I hauled ice and coal
and I followed the plow
many a day in the boiling hot sun
'cause when I got married
I worked a farm in the delta
and become a sharecropper;
but the white folks took all I made
and kept me heavy in they debt
and ain't nary one of my babies went to school
and my wife, she half-starved
and died with consumption.

MARGARET WALKER

But fifteen years ago, on Monday morning the quiet, dusty, shady streets would be full of Negro women with, balanced on their steady, turbaned heads, bundles of clothes tied up in sheets, almost as large as cotton bales, carried so without touch of hand between the kitchen door of the white house and the blackened washpot beside a cabin door in Negro Hollow.

Nancy would set her bundle on the top of her head, then upon the bundle in turn she would set the black straw sailor hat which she wore winter and summer. She was tall, with a high, sad face sunken a little where her teeth were missing. Sometimes we would go a part of the way down the lane and across the pasture with her, to watch the balanced bundle and the hat that never bobbed nor wavered, even when she walked down in the ditch and up the other side and stooped through the fence. She would go down on her hands and knees and crawl through the gap, her head rigid, uptilted, the bundle steady as a rock or a balloon, and rise to her feet again and go on.

WILLIAM FAULKNER

Her eyes are diamonds of pure dark space
& the air flying out of them as you look
close is only the essence of living
to tell, a full-length woman, an aunt
brown & red with stalking the years

AL YOUNG

. . . remember the firstborn who died
                              without her births rite?

she rolls my mothers
memory
in the mississippi dust

my father plucks and knocks her hidden bones
                                    roots now.

where
time falls and
            fails
beneath the central soil.

we are not defeated.

ANGELA JACKSON

Sugars and resin, grain
By grain, burn toward their lees;
And where two smokes, one cane,
One pine, drift in the trees,

Dark residues foretell
Our season's heritage—
Where, through time's circling smell,
The slow mule plods toward age.

TURNER CASSITY

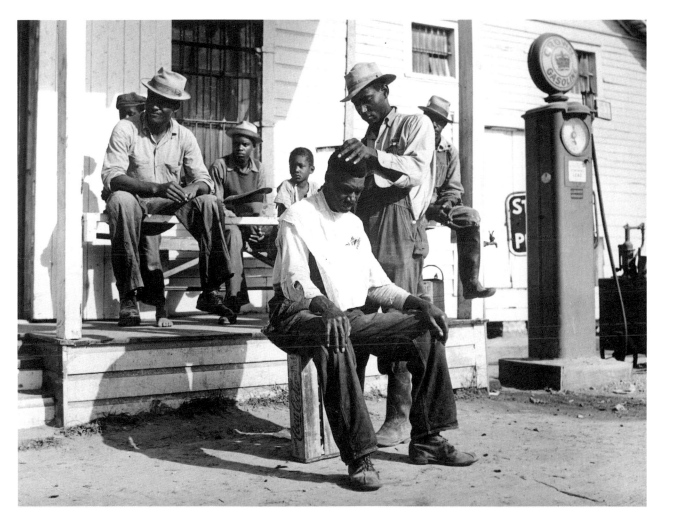

Levitt: That's right, the late twenties. 'Twenty-seven, 'twenty-eight. And the Depression was already on as far as I was concerned—as far as the *South* was concerned. Poor people in the South never did much good in my lifetime. Even rich people weren't all *that* rich. So I came back here and farmed. Cut pulpwood. Did daywork when I could get it. Turned my hand to anything I could get. It was *root, hog, or die.*

ELLEN DOUGLAS

The parlor might have belonged to another family. The two rooms shared a chimney, but, unless there was company in the house, the parlor grate was cold. It was a cold room, cold and uncomfortable, its furniture too small and fragile—Victorian love seats and straight-backed chairs with legs that had been broken again and again by big men who tilted back and stretched out their legs in an effort to make themselves comfortable. Starched white doilies protected the table tops and were scattered like big snowflakes on the arms and backs of the chairs, and cold, gray velvet hung at the windows. In spite of its gloom and shabbiness, the dining room vibrated with the life of the family, and in spite of its effort at elegance, the parlor had no life at all. . . .

She was tired of courting in the parlor, and she listened to the murmur of voices on the other side of the wall and wished that just one evening she and Ralph could change sides with the family. If they could get comfortable . . . She knew herself to be helpless within the limits of courtship against his ingrained formality, and she could think of nothing to do about it. *Nobody can help me, and there's no use blaming it on the parlor*, she thought to herself.

E L L E N   D O U G L A S

STANLEY: Then where's the money if the place was
   sold?

STELLA: Not sold— *lost, lost!*

TENNESSEE WILLIAMS

In the nineteenth century the cotton growers, adventurous younger sons and brothers, came here from the older South where the land had played out, seeking the rich alluvial earth. Later the merchants came to exploit the commerce of the Yazoo River, where the old river boats were stacked ten and fifteen deep in cotton bales, and steamboats with names like the *Hard Cash*, the *City of Greenwood*, and the *Katie Robbins* plied their trade from the upper delta to Vicksburg. Keel- and flatboats laden with flour and apples started out on the Yazoo River, then entered the Mississippi and went all the way south to New Orleans. These early settlers had names like Beatty, Adams, Bull, Clark, Gray, Howard, Little, Robertson, Sparks, Taylor, Thompson, Walton, Whitehead, Young. The slaves had the names of the masters, and for years the tax lists of the place suggested the old Anglo-Saxon blood-source. Later others came to this lower delta—Italians, Irish, Jews, Syrians, even Chinese—to produce a curious melting pot, black, yellow, and white, and all the gradations known to man.

WILLIE MORRIS

III

I practically grew up in this graveyard, and as children we came here for picnics and games, wandering among the graves on our own, with no adults about, watching the funerals from afar in a hushed awe, and I believe that was when I became obsessed not with death itself but with the singular community of death and life together—and life's secrets, life's fears, life's surprises.

WILLIE MORRIS

We had a population made up for the most part of Anglo-Saxons and blacks, although a scattering of Jewish and Italian and Greek residents, with one Belgian and one Creole from New Orleans, added spice to the mixture. We had our village atheist and a couple of village drug addicts—"dope fiends" as we rather inelegantly and perhaps a bit melodramatically referred to them in those days before euphemism became a national pastime—one of them the scion of a pioneer family of the area, whose particular devotion was, I recall, to paregoric. We also had our village Republican, just one, the father of a classmate and friend of mine, who cast Tupelo's sole vote for Thomas Dewey in the 1948 election, thereby aligning himself, for all those who knew his identity, with the camp of the dope fiends and the atheist. We had our fair share of eccentrics—men and women—those non-conformists who contribute to a town, if nothing else, an endless source of conversation, or, if you will, gossip. There was a man who claimed to have created fried bananas as a dish; a woman who insisted that she had drunk no water for twenty years, having survived exclusively on Coca Cola; another woman who professed to know government secrets and to be, as a result, the target of Communist agents. We had piano teachers, Avon ladies, Fuller brush men, insurance salesmen, wife beaters, a couple of kleptomaniacs, one flasher, one woman who had tried out for the part of Scarlett O'Hara, a score of inveterate liars; four bootleggers, one of them a woman, and several fortune tellers, who worked out of their homes.

KENNETH HOLDITCH

MEG: Why, you're just as perfectly sane as anyone walking the streets of Hazlehurst, Mississippi.

BETH HENLEY

It was here under the water oaks that his father used to stroll of a summer night, hands in his pockets and head down, sauntering along the sidewalk in his old Princeton style of sauntering, right side turning forward with right leg. Here under the water oaks or there under the street light, he would hold parley with passers-by, stranger and friend, white and black, thief and police.

WALKER PERCY

PHOTO BY HANNA.

DIVELBISS BOOK STORE.

It must have been
something like Farish
Street in the bebop for-
ties, a ragtag holy ghost
baptizing Mississippi
on an unexpected
Sunday, . . .
Jerry W. Ward, Jr.

But above all, the courthouse: the center, the focus, the hub; sitting looming in the center of the county's circumference like a single cloud in its ring of horizon, laying its vast shadow to the uttermost rim of horizon; musing, brooding, symbolic and ponderable, tall as cloud, solid as rock, dominating all.

WILLIAM FAULKNER

So there were railroads in the land now; now couples who had used to go overland by carriage to the River landings and the steamboats for the traditional New Orleans honeymoon, could take the train from almost anywhere. And presently pullmans too, all the way from Chicago and the Northern cities where the cash, the money was, so that the rich Northerners could come down in comfort and open the land indeed: setting up with their Yankee dollars the vast lumbering plants and mills in the southern pine section, the little towns which had been hamlets without change or alteration for fifty years, booming and soaring into cities overnight above the stump-pocked barrens which would remain until in simple economic desperation people taught themselves to farm pine trees as in other sections they had already learned to farm corn and cotton.

WILLIAM FAULKNER

Bareheaded and barefooted, my brother and I, along with nameless and countless other black children, used to stand and watch the men crawl in, out, over, and under the huge black metal engines. When the men were not looking, we would climb into the engineer's cab and pull our small bodies to the window and look out, imagining that we were grown and had got a job as an engineer running a train and that it was night and there was a storm and we had a long string of passenger cars behind us, trying to get them safely home.

RICHARD WRIGHT

The roads they built were local affairs, connecting plantation with plantation or with hamlets which grew slowly and without booms into our present small towns. In wet weather, of which we have much, they were bottomless, and old-timers believed they could never be anything else.

WILLIAM ALEXANDER PERCY

Poppa had to drive slowly for the first quarter of a mile from the station, because we'd be passing Miss Spencer's mansion. In addition to her being a white woman, she was known as a reckless driver, and we had the responsibility to ensure that if she came out of her driveway in her Duesenberg without stopping, she'd have plenty of room.

CLIFTON TAULBERT

On a winter afternoon, unseasonably warm, a car was racing over country roads toward town. Dust, gushing from the back wheels, ran together behind in a dense whirl. On the headlands, the sun cast its thin glare above the sagebrush; it shot through the little trees, the pin oaks and the new reedy pines, and its touch pained the eye. . . .

One thing about the car: it knew the road. A country car, after a few months of driving have loosened every joint and axle and worn the shock absorbers tender and given every part a special cry of its own, pushes very fine the barrier that divides it from horses and mules. The road it knows, it navigates: dodges the washouts, straddles the ruts, nicks the bumps on the easy corner, and strikes, just at the point of balance, the loose plank in the bridge.

ELIZABETH SPENCER

The bridge was a fine one for such a small bayou. It was a drawbridge with high steel girders that gleamed like silver in the flat Delta countryside. The bridge had been built to connect the two parts of the county, and anyone going from Grace to Baleshed or Esperanza or Panther Brake or Greenfields had to pass that way. Some mornings as many as seven cars and trucks passed over it. All day small black children played on the bridge and fished from it and leaned over its railings looking down into the brown water, chunking rocks at the mud turtles or trying to hit the mean-looking gars and catfish that swam by in twos or threes with their teeth showing.

ELLEN GILCHRIST

129

CARNELLE: Well, Delmount, I don't know! I've never thought about leaving Brookhaven.

DELMOUNT: Well, think about it. There's never been anything here for you but sorrow.

CARNELLE: Yes, that's true. Still . . . I don't know. (*After a moment*) Maybe if I could, if I could leave in a blaze of glory. Yes! That's what I'd like to do—leave this town in a blaze of glory!

BETH HENLEY

THE PHOTOGRAPHS

The photographs are from seventeen collections in the Mississippi Archives library.

Chamberlain-Hunt Collection—photographs dating from 1885 of Chamberlain-Hunt Academy of Port Gibson

Coovert Collection—photographs made by J. C. Coovert, a professional photographer living in Greenville, Mississippi, in the 1890s; his Mississippi images show scenes in Greenville, Vicksburg, Yazoo City, Memphis, and Jackson.

Daniel Collection—photographs made by Albert Frederick Daniel, who operated a photography studio in Jackson from 1905 to 1935

Doolittle Family Collection—photographs collected by members of the Doolittle family who lived in the community of Doolittle, near Newton, Mississippi

East Collection—photographs dating from 1867 collected by Charles East, writer and editor, originally from Shelby, Mississippi

Elliot Collection—photographs collected by Jack Elliot, Jr., in the West Point, Mississippi, vicinity

Elms Collection—photographs from the Elms, Natchez, Mississippi, ca. 1900

FSA Collection—photographs made by photographers employed by the Farm Security Administration to document rural life in the United States in the 1930s and 1940s; photographers include Dorothea Lange, Russell Lee, Carl Mydans, Arthur Rothstein, and Marion Post Wolcott.

Lampton Family Papers—family photographs from Thaddeus Boothe Lampton, Tylertown businessman, and his descendants

Painter Collection—photographs made by the photographer Milton McFarland Painter between 1912 and 1930; Painter, who was born in 1878 in Water Valley, Mississippi, lived in Friar's Point and Clarksdale.

Piney Woods Country Life School Records—photographs dating from 1930 from the Piney Woods Country Life School

Post Card Collection—postcards of Mississippi scenes donated by the State Historical Society of Wisconsin

Stewart Collection—photographs made by Robert Livingston Stewart of Natchez about 1890–1900, from 8 × 10 glass negatives

Von Seutter Collection—photographs from the von Seutter family of Jackson; Emil von Seutter was a German emigré who established a jewelry store in Jackson in 1851.

WPA Collection—photographs from the 1930s by the Works Progress Administration

Wells Collection—family photographs collected by Mrs. W. W. Wells of Heidelburg, Mississippi, including images from the town Newton and from Jasper and Forrest counties

Williams Collection—photographs related to the evangelical career of Howard S. Williams of Hattiesburg; Williams was a journalist who worked at the Jackson *Daily News* and owned the *Hattiesburg American* before traveling throughout the country as an evangelist.

Photograph captions below include information as documented at the Department of Archives and History and indicate collections in which the photographs are found.